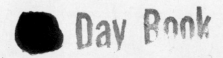

Meet the Real Pilgrims

Meet the Real Pilgrims,

Everyday Life on
Plimoth Plantation in 1627

by Robert H. Loeb, Jr.

IN CONSULTATION WITH PLIMOTH PLANTATION

DOUBLEDAY & COMPANY, INC.
GARDEN CITY, NEW YORK

PHOTO CREDITS
All photographs are reproduced here by courtesy of Plimoth Plantation.

Library of Congress Cataloging in Publication Data

Loeb, Robert H
Meet the real pilgrims.

SUMMARY: Describes everyday life in a replica of
the 17th-century community and presents interviews
with men and women who speak Elizabethan English
and live as the original settlers did.
    1. Pilgrims (New Plymouth Colony)—Juvenile
literature. 2. Massachusetts—History—New Colonial period, 1600- 177
Plymouth, 1620–1691—Juvenile literature. [1. Pil-
grims (New Plymouth Colony) 2. Massachusetts—
History—New Plymouth, 1620–1691] I. Plimoth
Plantation, inc. Plymouth, Mass. II. Title.
        F68.L83   974.4′02   L8222 mv
    ISBN: 0-385-14152-1 Trade
        0-385-14153-x Prebound
Library of Congress Catalog Card Number 78–1208

×1. Pilgrims (New England
    Colonists)

ACKNOWLEDGMENTS

I wish to thank the staff of Plimoth Plantation in working with me on *Meet the* Real *Pilgrims*. My thanks are especially extended to James Deetz for his initial interest, to James Baker for historical guidance, to Bill Martin for his Elizabethan linguistics, and to Pat Kamlin for co-ordinating the project.

A NOTE FROM THE AUTHOR

In preparing to be your guide for this tour through seventeenth-century Plimoth, I spent some time inspecting the present village of Plimoth Plantation. It is a working replica of Plimoth as it was in 1627. The fort, houses, and other buildings have been constructed to duplicate, in most instances, Plimoth Plantation as it originally was. The men and women who "live" in the village dress as the original villagers did and farm and cook as people did in the seventeenth century. They even talk as the original settlers did—in Elizabethan English. However, they only live in the village from nine to five and are called *interpreters*. They are like actors playing their assigned parts, in dress, speech, and activities. I interviewed some of them and taped their dialogue. By so doing, I learned, at first hand, how some of the citizens of Plimoth felt, thought, and lived.

It is important, then, to realize that all of the dialogue in *Meet the* Real *Pilgrims* consists of direct quotations from my interviews and is not my creation. Furthermore, the dialogue and its spelling were carefully checked in order to duplicate, as authentically as possible, the vernacular of the seventeenth century.

R.H.L.

Contents

Meet the Real Pilgrims

Approach to the fort

CHAPTER 1

Meet the Real *Pilgrims*

Let me introduce myself. I am going to be your guide during your visit to Plimoth Plantation. And I hope you'll think of me as your friend as well. Because, when we continue walking down this path and enter the plantation, I think you'll want someone who is familiar to you. For you'll be entering a most unfamiliar world, the world as it was over three hundred and fifty years ago, in 1627.

You're probably already puzzled as to why the plantation's name, Plimoth, is spelled with an *i* rather than with a *y* and without a *u*. That's because William Bradford, who was the plantation's governor for many years and its first historian, spelled it "Plimoth" rather than "Plymouth." Even spelling in those early times was very different.

Straight ahead of us, behind the fort and wooden wall, called a *palisade,* live one hundred and fifty-six men, women, and children whose customs, way of life, beliefs, and even whose way of talking will seem strange to you.

I suspect, however, that you are thinking: "I already know about the Pilgrims. Who doesn't? They came over on the *Mayflower,* landed at Plymouth Rock, and all that."

Well, you are in for some surprises. In the first place, the people living here don't call themselves *Pilgrims.* The word comes from the Bible and refers to people who journeyed to the Holy Land. In his history book, Governor Bradford did call those who came over on the *Mayflower* with him "Pilgrims." That's because he felt, or hoped, that they had journeyed to a new kind of Holy Land where they would have freedom of worship. However, the settlers never referred to themselves as "Pilgrims." About one hundred years later, Cotton Mather, a Congregational minister in Boston, called the early settlers of Plimoth "Pilgrims" in one of his books. The name was picked up in the latter part of the eighteenth century, in a popular poem about the founding of Plimoth, and from then on, the term became commonly used.

Another surprise may be that the majority of people in Plimoth did not come over on the *Mayflower.* Of the one hundred and two *Mayflower* passengers, over half of them died during their first winter here in 1620. Since that time, nine more ships arrived from England, with additional settlers.

Starting with the *Mayflower* passengers, why did these English people continue coming to the New World? It's important to know this so that you'll have an understanding of those you're going to meet. Poverty was the chief reason why most of these settlers decided to risk the unknown dangers of the New World wilderness. The great majority of people living in England and on the Continent in the 1620s were very poor. In addition, some of them sought to escape religious persecution and to be able to worship in the manner they believed to be the proper Christian way. This minority group are called *Separatists*. The reason they are referred to as "Separatists" requires a bit of explanation.

It's disturbing to realize that Christianity, which was supposed to make people love and respect each other, often has been the cause of frightful discord and cruel intolerance. This is precisely what happened to some men and women in Queen Elizabeth I's and James I's reigns some forty years before. Both these monarchs were fanatical about maintaining the Church of England—the Anglican Church—as the only permissible religion. Some English people objected to its fancy pomp and ceremony which seemed to them too much like the Roman Catholic Church. Furthermore, they felt that some of the Church of England's clergy were far more interested in accumulating power and wealth than in carrying out Christ's teachings. These objectors wished to "purify" the Church and became known as *Puritans*. The majority of them tried to reform the Established Church by working from within it. But other Puritans felt that the only way they could bring about change was to establish their own, separate places of worship. This group became known as "Separatists."

Queen Elizabeth had been ruthless to anyone who

defied the Church. Catholic, Puritan—in fact anyone suspected of religious deviance was imprisoned, sometimes tortured, and even hanged. King James, who was the settlers' ruler until two years earlier, carried on in the same repressive way. The Separatists, especially, were continually threatened, some fined and others imprisoned. Consequently they found it dangerous to worship in their meetinghouses. A determined band of them moved to the city of Amsterdam, in Holland, the only country in the entire Christian world which permitted freedom of worship. Some other English Separatists were already there. Unfortunately, religious differences arose between the two groups and some decided to move to another Dutch city, Leyden. They stayed there from 1609 to 1620.

In Leyden they enjoyed freedom of worship. But living conditions were even worse than back in England. Although accustomed to working long hours, they had to work and slave even harder in Leyden in order to barely survive. It was common practice, among poor people then, to put their children to work by the time they were six or seven years old. But in Leyden their children had to work such long hours that the parents felt their health was threatened. Furthermore, the grown-ups really didn't like living among foreigners and having their children speak Dutch.

That's when they decided to emigrate to the New World, America. There, they hoped they would be among other English people, enjoy a better standard of living, and have freedom of worship as well. But there was a hitch: to make this drastic move required money, precisely what they didn't have. They needed money to buy or charter ships to take them across the Atlantic and to stock the ships with food, livestock, tools, weapons, and other supplies.

They had some friends and agents in London who set about trying to raise funds. After many refusals the agents approached a Thomas Weston. He was a promoter of risky business ventures. He set up a company of wealthy merchants who were looking for ways to invest their money as profitably as possible. They called themselves the *adventurers,* which means "speculators." They were not in the least interested in helping needy or persecuted people. Consequently, they drove a hard bargain. The Separatists and the non-Separatists who were going with them thought they had a workable understanding with the adventurers. They agreed that they would set up a plantation which would be owned jointly with the adventurers for seven years. All profits from fishing, farming, and the Indian trade would be shared equally during that period. But they assumed that the homes they would build and the gardens and fields they would cultivate would surely belong to them.

Shortly before departure time, the adventurers presented the hopeful voyagers with an agreement to sign. It stated that *all* plantation property, including homes and gardens, would belong to the company until the money lent was paid back. One ship, the *Speedwell,* had already been bought. And when the *Mayflower* was chartered and its owner paid, the planters had used up all monies advanced to them and needed more for further provisions. Nevertheless, they refused to sign the

The *Mayflower*

agreement. Instead, they sold some of their less necessary supplies and raised the additional funds needed to set sail.

The *Speedwell* left Leyden with the Separatists aboard on July 22, joining up with the *Mayflower* at Southampton. Both ships set forth on August 15, but twice the *Speedwell* developed leaks and the two ships returned for repairs first to Dartmouth and then to Plymouth. The *Speedwell* was deemed unseaworthy, so some of its passengers transferred to the *Mayflower,* while the others stayed aboard the *Speedwell* and proceeded to London. Overcrowded with one hundred and two passengers and a crew of twenty-five, the *Mayflower* finally sailed on September 16, 1620, from Plymouth. Of the passengers, forty were Separatists and sixty-two non-Separatists who had been recruited from London and nearby by the adventurers. Though of different faiths, the two groups shared a common goal: the hope of improving their living conditions and of giving their children a better world to grow up in than they had in England.

It is for all these reasons that these English people emigrated to the New World and founded Plimoth Plantation in 1620. We are now going to go back in time and visit the colony as it was seven years later, in 1627.

View from the fort

CHAPTER **2**

Welcome to Plimoth

First let's climb to the gun deck on top of the fort and look at the entire village. The view from up here shows us how the town is laid out. The palisade encloses it in more of a diamond shape than a square. It's only twenty-seven hundred feet in circumference and the town barely covers an acre of ground. It was designed in accordance with plans of fortified towns in northern Ireland.

The main street extends through the middle of town from directly below us to the furthermost end at the seashore. It's intersected at the center by a cross street. The houses, as you can see, line both sides of the main street and each has a small, fenced-in garden at the rear. At the point where the streets intersect you can see a tiny square structure. It looks like a mini-fort, which is exactly what it is. Inside it are four small *ordnances* (cannons) mounted on swivels. They are easy to reload and fire a spread of small shot which can be rapidly aimed down both streets. Their purpose is to repel any rebellion within the town. I am happy to say, however, that the governor has never had to use them. The people live peaceably together although there has been, and probably still is, some dissatisfaction on the part of a few citizens.

But now enough of viewing from the top. Let's step into this fascinating world of the past and experience it as it really is, both the good and the bad.

We've entered Plimoth through the west gate, at the beginning of what's called "the street." You probably didn't expect to see cars, buses, or trucks roaring up and down. But you may be disappointed that there are neither horse-drawn carriages nor anyone trotting or cantering about on horseback. With the exception of some pigs rooting and shuffling about, some sheep, and a few little children at the farther end, the street does look quite deserted.

You see, carriages other than carts and crude wagons are mostly unknown now even in England. And at the present time there's not a single horse at the Plantation, although I understand that a few may be shipped over shortly. The settlers go about on foot, and when they need to plow their fields, they hitch up a steer or dry cow. It's not an ideal solution, but then, the great majority of these people didn't own a horse, let alone a yoke of oxen, back in England.

Another reason why the street is so quiet is because it's still a bit before noon. The men are undoubtedly working in the fields. Everyone, including the governor himself, spends most of the time farming outside the palisade. The women pitch in, too, but at this hour they're probably busy indoors preparing the noonday meal and tending to the various other chores.

As for the pigs you see, the settlers are accustomed to them roaming about the street. Pigs are their main source of meat as cattle and goats are in short supply. Most of the pigs are herded out into the fields to feed on stubble. Sometimes they're even herded down to the seashore below, to feed on shellfish at low tide. No one, however, minds the stragglers, as long as they don't get into the herb and vegetable gardens behind the houses. I suspect, too, that the pigs may serve as four-footed garbage collectors.

The reason there are no older children romping and playing about is not because they're at school. There is no school of any kind at Plimoth. And I happen to know that there won't be one until 1671, which is a long way off. And it won't be much of a school at that, because public education and regular school attendance, as you know it only too well, will not be established in America until the middle of the nineteenth century. How then do children pass the time? There's no TV to gape at, no radio, movies, comics, Little League. The answer is: they're put to work. By the time they're six or seven, children are considered mini-adults, not helpless, tender creatures needing coddling and protection. And they wear the same kind of clothing as grown-ups. Even so, they're expected to do as they're told and are not to show any sense of independence. Stubbornness and willfulness are not tolerated. Complete and unquestioning obedience is the rule. This undoubtedly goes

Pigs roaming

against the beliefs of modern child psychologists. But I don't think you'll find the children here less happy or less well-adjusted than those in our world.

You'll have plenty of opportunity to find out, because, oddly enough, almost half the population— seventy-three—are children, the majority of them below their teens.

I'm sure you're becoming more and more curious to see where you'll be staying. John Billington's house is halfway down the street, on the right, just before we get to the intersection of the cross street. It's directly opposite Governor Bradford's far larger home. However, there's not a great deal of neighborliness between the two households.

Since you're going to be staying with John, I want to tell you a bit about him. First of all, the way he talks undoubtedly may seem quite odd. There are several reasons for that. In the first place, he, like everyone else here, talks a seventeenth-century English called "Elizabethan English." Secondly, because he, like almost everyone here, is completely uneducated, his grammar is not of the best.

In describing his relationship with the governor, he said to me recently: "I tell thou, though I've little trouble with goovnor, there's them that say *he* says I were born to be hung. Perhaps him bein' a country man he don't understand the ways of an Loondoner. And 'course he's one of them Separaytists, one o' the Saints, and they be runnin' it all for theyselves advantage."

His reference to the Separatists as "Saints" definitely

does not imply that John considers them especially good. The word *Saint,* as he uses it, means someone who is very dedicated to his religious faith, as are most of the Separatists. John and the other settlers who are not Separatists are called *Strangers.* The majority of the people in Plimoth are Strangers. They were recruited by the merchant adventurers and persuaded to come to this new land to improve their living conditions. They're not here for any religious reasons.

As John puts it: "I warn't doin' none so well in Loondon, hired to an merchant in Cheepside. So me and the family, we hears so mooch 'bout profit in the beaver fur trade and sooch like, and the plantin' of a colony would be the opportunity to fish and send a proportion of thot to the Loondon, or perhaps Bristol, market. I tell thou this: the fishin' venture nay work out. For many like meself have little experience fishin', many bein' inlanders with no experience 'pon the salt at all. So the fishin' hath come to nought. The fur trade, now, 'tis been a profit though I 'spect it to be some time fore we're clear of debt to the merchants."

(There is, I should point out, a third group of non-Separatists living here who are not indebted to the merchants in England. They have come over in the past few years and paid for their passage themselves. They are called the *Particulars.* However, all of them arrived here penniless. They landed with practically no proper clothing nor adequate supplies of any kind. How they thought they would get by in this new land so ill-provided is a mystery. The governor and his council wondered about that, too. But they decided that they could not let the Particulars freeze to death, so they supplied them with shelter, clothing, food, and tools to work with. Consequently, although the Particulars are not indebted to the merchants, they are indebted to Plimoth Plantation and have had to agree to share their portion of the over-all debt along with everyone else.)

Men such as Governor Bradford tend to look down upon John, not so much because he's not a member of the Separatist faith, but because he comes from the lower classes. Not that the governor is a member of the English aristocracy, but his father is a yeoman farmer back in England. This means he is a man of some property, since a yeoman farmer owns a certain amount of land. Though little in comparison to what the English landed gentry and the nobility own, a yeoman is his own master. The great majority of English people, on the other hand, own practically nothing and have to spend their lives working for others in order to survive. (That would have been John's lot if he hadn't come over here.)

Not only is the governor's father a man of modest means, but his mother was the daughter of the village shopkeeper which means they were not poor. Although the governor never had the advantage of a formal education, he has spent years educating himself. He knows his Bible by heart and owns a number of other books which he has read from cover to cover. Compared to John, therefore, he is extremely well educated. As a matter of fact, I happen to know that the governor is going to write a book in a few years about the history of the settling of Plimoth Plantation.

I asked John recently, "Can you read and write with ease?"

I put it that way to be polite as I suspected that he can do neither.

"Oh, I can read," he replied, "I read several words at an time. Thinks nothin' of it. 'Course I d'nay read like goovnor, nor sortainly not like Master Brewster, him what's head of the congregation. Now *he* readeth both Hebrew and Grake and he's tutorin' goovnor in Latin 'n sooch like. I be no learned scholar like he. He stoodied at Cambridge for an noomber of years. Yet I do read a bit. Wife, 'course she don't read nowt. We have the Bible in our house, but d'nay see everythin' in the Bible what goovnor sees."

I must say that John, like some of the other Strangers, tends to grumble about being discriminated against by the governor and the men he has chosen to run Plimoth, all of who are Separatists except for Captain Miles Standish. For example, just the other day John said: "I don't think them of us what ain't Saints are gettin' our fair proportion betimes. Been a long time since an Stranger were appointed assistant to goovnor. They run it all to theyselves. 'Course," he quickly added, "I don't want nothin' of this to get back to goovnor."

His critical attitude, though, seems quite unjustified. Just a few weeks ago Governor Bradford called a general meeting. It was only attended by the men twenty-one years or older. Those under twenty-one, according to English law, are considered children. And no women were allowed to be present. Women have no voice in politics. In fact, they have no legal rights of any kind. They, like children, are second-class citizens.

The reason the governor called the meeting was because a financial agreement had been worked out with the merchants in England. Bradford and his council agreed to purchase complete ownership of Plimoth Plantation from them. They were to pay the merchants £1,800 in nine annual installments. This sum is about one third of what the merchants invested in financing the settlement of the plantation and, in the 1970s, amounts to about $180,000. It seems that the merchants were willing to take a loss of $360,000 because they feared that, if they didn't accept the offer, they might never get back a penny on their investment.

The governor described the agreement at the meeting and explained that, as a result, the settlers now were the sole owners of the plantation, that everyone jointly owned all the land, the gardens, houses and all the livestock. But the big question to solve was, who owns what specifically and who would share in paying the $20,000 a year to the merchants? The way these problems were solved at the meeting makes John's complaints seem most unwarranted. For regardless of whether a man is a Separatist or not, even if he's a Particular, each of the fifty-eight men has received a one-share ownership of the plantation. And neither the governor nor the members of his council have received more. In addition, every man with a family, and there are twenty-one, has received one additional share for each member of his household. This means that John, who has a wife and son, Francis, owns three shares. This, in turn, means that John now possesses sixty-three acres of land as each share entitles the owner to twenty-one acres. Furthermore, he now owns his home. And to show you how truly fair the governor and council have been, those who do have larger homes—such as Bradford himself, William Brewster, Edward Winslow, and a few others —have agreed to pay an equalizing fee to men like John whose houses are far more modest.

That's why it's hard to understand why John complains as he does. Perhaps it's just his nature to grumble. As a matter of fact, when I asked him directly whether he didn't think he was better off than if he had remained in England, he said:

"Ay, there's land here. Only bloody gentlemen own land back in England. So I d'nay want ter go back to Loondon now."

I thought it would make good sense for you to stay at John's home because it represents the average household. Not only are the wealthier settlers' houses larger, but they have servants, which people like John do not have.

Here we are in front of the Billingtons' and you can really see how tiny the house actually is. It has only two rooms and a loft. The way this house is built is far different from what you're used to seeing. Take the roof, for example. It's not shingled, but covered with thatch. Thatch is made by arranging straw in parallel strands and then tying them together. Surprisingly enough, this form of roofing sheds rain just about as well as shingles do and outlasts them.

John Billington's house in winter

The house is sheathed with clapboard, which is commonly used in our modern world. But the clapboard is not painted. Each one of these clapboards was handmade by splitting a log lengthwise; then it was shaved down to the proper shape with a two-handled blade called a *drawknife*.

I'm certain that the chimney doesn't resemble any you have ever seen. It's made neither of stone, nor brick, nor cement. It looks, instead, as if it is made from clay which is partly so. The reason for its crude,

Thatching a roof

Making siding

flimsy construction is that John and the other settlers have had to work with what's at hand. The stones hereabouts are unusable as they're mostly round. And no one as yet has made bricks. The chimney was constructed with a wood framework. It was then filled, inside and out, with wattlework. This consists of slender boughs of wood which are woven together. Then they're covered on each side with clay. Such construction doesn't make for a very efficient chimney as the heat from the fire often cracks the clay. As a result, John has to reclay it several times a year. Surprisingly enough, however, chimney fires are not that frequent, chiefly be-

Building a chimney

cause the hearth fires are kept small. Huge, blazing fires would be a real hazard.

There are only two windows for the entire little house. And they're so small that, to you, they probably seem like peepholes. Each is only about ten inches square and has no glass pane. It's covered with oiled paper. Some of the houses don't even have this covering over their windows, but merely wooden shutters which are shut during cold weather. Winters here are long and cold as a rule. Therefore the fewer windows a house has, the more heat is retained inside. And the only heat there is comes from the fireplace, which is very little indeed.

Although John's house may seem more like a cabin, or even a shack, to you, he is well pleased with it. That's because most of the settlers were accustomed to a crude way of living in England.

"I ware responsible for the buildin' of it," John says proudly, "and I considers it an fair house. It's right comfortable. It hath *two* windows. The mistress, she d'nay like it, but she likes nothin' 'bout ther New World."

There's one thing I've got to prepare you for before John arrives, which should be at any moment. To put it frankly, you're going to find that he and his family, as well as everyone else here, smell. Especially when you're cooped up indoors with them. That's because they neither bathe nor wash. It's not because they're lazy. It's because they believe that scrubbing the body with soap and water is bad for one's health. To make matters worse, they only wash their clothing a few times a year. That's not because they believe that doing laundry is unhealthy. There is, instead, a somewhat understandable reason. The water needed for drinking, cooking, and laundry has to be carried all the way from the town brook which is beyond the palisade. Then, to have hot water for washing, it has to be heated in a huge iron pot suspended over the fire. That takes time and effort and there are so many things which these people must do in order to survive that something has to go. And since everyone smells about the same, it's unnoticeable to them.

I hope you're prepared for one additional, slight discomfort: there's no such thing as indoor plumbing. That includes toilet facilities. The outdoors is used instead, and that means outside the palisade regardless of weather. I'm sure, however, that you'll quickly get used to such somewhat superficial discomforts.

Well, here's John at last and he'll take us into the house and probably talk our ears off. But I'm sure you'll find this new experience in living fascinating.

CHAPTER 3

Noon at the Billingtons'

John's gone into the house to warn his wife that he's brought guests for dinner. I hope the news won't upset her. But it's time for us to find out, so let's enter.

It is dark in here, since very little light comes through the tiny window. In fact, more light is coming from the fireplace opening. And during the cold weather, when the door has to remain shut, it's even darker. But this does not bother the Billingtons. To them, it's normal indoor lighting, as it is in the other houses here. Besides, weather permitting, most of the settlers' daytime activities are spent outdoors.

Now that your eyes have become accustomed to the darkness you can see Helen Billington. She's busy before the fireplace where she's been cooking the midday meal.

Before we find out what we're going to eat, I'd like to point out some of the features of the house. We're in the main room, called the *hall*. Actually, it's the only real room, small as it is. The huge fireplace takes up a good portion of the entire area. Over on the right, at

Cooking in the fireplace

the rear, there is another room, if one can call it that. It's only six feet by eight and is called the *chamber*.

Look at the floor. If you think you're standing on nothing more than dirt, you're quite correct. It was made by first digging up the earth and crumbling it into little bits. Then it was soaked with water and stirred about so that it was like a huge mud pie. After that it was smoothed and carefully leveled like concrete flooring. After drying out, it became quite solid. However, with continual use, the surface gets scuffed and has to be patched with mud every so often. I must say that it looks as if John hasn't done much patching lately. Some of the homes cover the dirt surface with rushes to save wear and tear. Wooden floors are a luxury few of the houses have.

The fireplace not only takes up half the length of one wall, but is positively cavernous. It's three and a half feet deep and so high that even a tall person can walk into it. The back of it is lined with rounded stones set in clay. This lining extends only three feet up, but it's enough to protect the chimney wall from the heat of the fire. Looking up the chimney is a rather odd experience as it's really little more than a huge hole which goes through the roof and you can see the sky. As a result, most of the heat from the fire escapes out the roof and, worse yet, rain and snow come down into the hearth. This may seem crude, but it's a great improvement over the kinds of fireplaces used just a few years ago in England and, until recently, in some of the houses here at the plantation. They had no chimney of any sort. Instead, a gaping hole was made in the center of the roof beneath which a stone hearth was set. As you can imagine, more smoke remained in the room than escaped out the roof hole.

So it's understandable why John and even Helen, who seems hard to satisfy, are pleased with their comparatively modern heating and cooking facilities. Though when you see the work it takes to cook a meal in a fireplace, you may wonder why. The inside of the fireplace is cluttered with iron hooks, bars, and chains. These are suspended from a wooden beam, called a *lug pole,* which is up in the chimney stack beyond reach of the fire. The hooks and chains are needed for hanging the cooking pots. Soups, stews, and vegetables are cooked in big, heavy iron pots.

Today, for a main course, Helen has roasted some goat's meat, one of John's favorite foods. The roasting is done on a *spit,* the thin, iron rod with a handle at one end, which is close to the flames. It has to be turned quite often so that the meat doesn't burn. On a hot summer's day, tending the spit is not exactly a pleasant chore. And there's always the danger of burning your hand unless you're careful. Manipulating the heavy iron pots also has its hazards, and I don't doubt that many a cook is sometimes scalded or burned.

Helen baked the bread for today's dinner in an outdoor communal oven early this morning. Her bread has a very different taste and texture compared to the kind we're used to in the 1970s. It's made by combining wheat and rye flour, and Helen may have added a bit of ground corn meal as well. By the end of winter, when most of their supplies of grain have been used up, ground dried peas and beans are sometimes added to the dough as a filler. Although Helen's bread will undoubtedly taste rather odd, it's far more nutritious than the commonly used commercial breads modern Americans eat.

The noonday meal we're about to be served is the main one of the day. Along with meat, chicken, or fish, there's a good variety of vegetables and salad greens. During the winter months, when fresh vegetables are not available, the settlers eat dried and pickled ones. What with a plentiful supply of freshly churned butter and homemade cheeses, the settlers eat well. It has been estimated that from springtime through the harvest season, the average grown-up eats the following amounts each day:

One-half pound of butter or cheese
One-half pound of meat or fish
One-fourth pound of porridge meal, usually oatmeal
One pound of bread
One gallon of skimmed milk, whey, or beer
Fair amounts of fresh fruits and vegetables

Although such a diet consists of a lot of carbohydrates and is loaded with calories, these people are so active during the day that it suits them well. I doubt if you'll see any fat people around here whereas one third of modern-day Americans are overweight from faulty diets and little exercise.

"We eat mooch better than if one's ever lived in Loondon," John says. "The food 'ere's mooch the better than thot we 'ad in Loondon. We raise good salad greens and we've got store of yarbs [herbs] in the yards 'hind our 'ouses."

During November and December the settlers have their best supply of fresh meats. However, very little beef is eaten. There are only a dozen or so cows and they're needed to supply the milk. What few steers they have are used for plowing and hauling. Heifers (young cows) and bulls are kept for breeding purposes. Although mutton is sometimes eaten, sheep are still scarce.

Pork, their main meat, is served fresh during slaughtering time, and, to preserve it for the rest of the year, it's first smoked and salted. Then it's usually pickled or made into sausage. Sometimes the salted pork is put into earthernware pots, covered with fat, and then sealed with a flour paste. Occasionally, after long storage, their meats become somewhat rancid. To disguise the unpleasant taste, they use lots of seasoned gravies.

There's also a plentiful supply of chickens, which are usually boiled rather than roasted. And there are lots of rabbits hopping about the countryside and they are among the settlers' favorite fresh meat.

John describes the main meal: "For dinner we've diverse things. 'Course oftentimes, in summer and early fall, we've herrin' what we take from the town brook. We preserves a proportion o' that for the time before slaughterin' comes 'round. We can slaughter pigs later on. We'll have pork, a good store o' that. We preserves many foods. We've preserved fruits, dryin' 'em, and we've salted herrin'. And then thou can, after a manner, rejuvenate dried herrin' after it's salted and hangin' in chimney and smoked out. It will stay very good and potentially sweet for a noomber of months. And when thou wish to use it, drop it in bylin' water and it be ready to eat. I prefers goat meself. We've many chickens, though, and good store of dooks and geese when we can gett'em."

His dislike of some seafood, which people today consider a delicacy, will surprise you:

"One thing I down't like very mooch are these clams we gather 'long seashore. They're times in past when we'd nommat to eat but clams and lobster and sooch. Mostly now we cooks lobster up and use them for bait in our eel traps. Now eel, that's a fine English dish which we 'as, too.''

Salads are popular during the summer and early fall, and they're served with a dressing of vinegar and olive oil, both of which come from overseas. There are no apple trees, except for wild crab apple, so neither vinegar nor cider can be made here.

You'll undoubtedly miss sugar or sweetening of any kind in the food here. Sugar also has to be shipped from England and it's very expensive. So it's used sparingly. And the settlers don't raise bees so there's no honey. However, the infrequent use of sugar is all to the good, since overuse of sugar may be harmful.

And don't be surprised if there's no cow's milk to drink at mealtime. It's rarely served, even to children. Almost all the milk is made into salted butter and cheese. Without refrigeration it's impossible to keep milk from spoiling, especially during the warm weather. Making it into butter and cheese solves this problem. Some drink goat's milk or skimmed milk or whey. Whey is the liquid left over after cheese is made. Their main drink is beer. The Billingtons and the other families make their own every few weeks. Beer is made from barley to which they add hops and then boil into a brew. It's called *small beer* and it contains very little alcohol. They also make another kind of beer that is aged for several months. It's alcoholic content is greater.

Dinner seems about ready. However, you're probably wondering where we're going to eat. No table has been set. In fact, there's no table to be seen for the simple

A noonday meal

reason that there's no room for one. Instead, Helen and Francis are removing a long board, which was set against the wall, and are placing it on top of two barrels. It serves as a table. There's an expression which has survived to modern times: "Being provided with bed and board." It means being given a place to sleep and meals, "board" referring to what the meals are served on.

As for seating arrangements, notice that there's only one chair. It's going to be used by none other than the master of the house, John Billington. A wooden chest, which can barely seat two, and a box are for the rest of us to sit on. This means that one person is going to have to eat standing up, a common practice. Dining is not exactly a formal occasion, but rather a refueling operation.

Setting the table is remarkably easy. There's practically nothing to set. Forks are an unknown utensil, both here and in England (though I do understand that the French upper class have them). Only a few wooden and pewter spoons are set out. They're used only as a last resort: for soup, porridge, or pudding which can't be eaten any other way. And by that I mean that they cannot be eaten with your hands. For hands are the main eating implements.

Note, too, that nothing resembling plates has been set on the board. Instead, Helen has placed hollowed-out wooden slabs for each of us. They are called *trenchers* and serve the same purpose. Not too many years ago most commoners in England used scooped-out pieces of their hard rye bread to place their food on, and the trenchers were modeled after them.

Where are the glasses or cups to drink from? There are none. Instead, there's a two-handled bowl that will be shared by all. Some of the wealthier households use individual beakers—large-sized drinking cups—and some even provide cups with handles. But the Billingtons and most of the other families at Plimoth don't own such fancy tableware.

A sharp knife is a must for each person. It's used to cut your slice of meat, cheese, bread, and butter. Thus dining involves knife and fingers. You will find that eating with your hands is quite a messy affair, especially with salad and vegetables. But, at least, napkins have been provided, which are as large as towels. They're a yard square, yet none too large at that. Because you'll need every inch to wipe hands and fingers on and to protect your clothing. But don't expect a clean one to be provided at each meal—or each day, for that matter. Laundry, as you already know, is done infrequently.

Now that we're gathered around the board, the smallness of the hall becomes even more obvious. With all the clutter of barrels, sacks of grain, tools, trunks, and all kinds of odds and ends stacked against the walls, we're ringed in. That's why, at the end of the meal, the board has to be dismantled, the chest and barrels set aside, so there will be room to move about.

Imagine what it's like for larger families where there are four or five children and everyone is cooped up in such a small space. Especially during the winter months when there's no escaping to the outdoors. There's practically no room for the little children to crawl about and play. Everyone is on top of one another, so that there's no such thing as privacy. One might think that this would lead to frequent squabbles and friction in the home. But, to the best of my knowledge, this is not the case. On the other hand, I am told that the men, especially, sometimes take out their sense of frustration by bickering with neighbors. But when this gets out of hand, the chief culprit is brought to trial before the governor and his council and is punished. As a result, order is well kept in the plantation. And there's less tension, certainly far less violence, among these people compared to ours today. After all, almost everyone is thankful that he or she no longer has to worry about having proper shelter and enough to eat. And the Separatists appreciate the fact that they may practice the religion of their choice.

True, day-to-day living can be rough. It involves a good deal of work which is sometimes frustrating, monotonous, and may not always be that rewarding. But a sense of humor often helps to make it endurable. As an amusing example, this is what John told me recently:

"The other day I had hard mornin'. I be thinkin' 'bout gettin' oop and the wife, she were fast asleep, and I d'nay want to waken her. She's of a temperament in mornin'. But I figur she'll have breakfast ready for I when I coom back and I goes out and I finds cow and I milches her. And I were carryin' two bookets o' milk back to house. Then I looks inter chamber and there she still be fast asleep and there be no fire in fireplace. And no oatmeal nor nommat for I to break-fast. I weren't very happy 'bout that. For milchin' cow ain't sooch an interestin' thing, not sooch a pleasant thing, early hour in the mornin'. I be quite hungry and I'm quite put out by this. So I call in the chamber and shouts, 'FIRE, FIRE FIRE!'

"She joomps right out o' bed like shot out 'o cannon 'n' cooms flyin' out o' chamber in her shift, callin': 'Where, where, where?'

"And I says: 'In everyone's hearth but thine!' "

Thus John made a joke out of an annoying situation. Although he did say that Helen didn't think it was very funny.

Dinner over and before we go outside, let's look at

the rest of the house, what little there is of it. The ladder leaning against the wall is used for climbing up to the loft. The loft covers less than half the area of the house. It's used for storing grain sacks and whatever else cannot be stored down here. It could be used for sleeping space. But it's so cluttered that even a cat would have trouble finding room to stretch out in.

The tiny doorless room off the hall is the chamber where John and Helen sleep. It has enough space for the one and only bed in the home and a chest. The bed has rope webbing rather than springs to support the mattress. The mattress is nothing more than a big sack filled with scraps of cloth. Some people have mattresses stuffed with raw wool and a few have them filled with feathers.

Since John and Helen sleep in the chamber and there's no space in the loft, where does their son, Francis, sleep? And, for that matter, where will you sleep? And on what? I hope this won't come as too much of a shock, for you and he are going to sleep in the hall on the floor. And you'll share a straw mattress. That's how children and servants are provided for. But you'll have a pillow, linen sheets, a blanket, plus a heavy covering on top of that. It's called a *rug* and sometimes referred to as a *coverlet* or *quilt*. When the sheets were last washed we won't think about, but you certainly won't be cold, though the floor is frightfully drafty.

Everyone goes to bed shortly after supper, which is served between seven and eight o'clock. There's not much else to do after eating, since there's neither much light nor room to do anything in. Nighttime illumination comes mainly from the fire. Candles are far too expensive to use except on very special occasions. And the two crude oil lamps shed scarcely any light.

You'll be getting up very early, along with the rest of the family. I don't imagine that Helen oversleeps anymore. And by "early" I mean at the crack of dawn. That's when the roosters start crowing and they serve as everyone's alarm clock.

Meanwhile, we have the entire afternoon ahead of us. Therefore let's go out and learn more about how the settlers live and work and what some others may have to say about life in Plimoth Plantation.

CHAPTER 4

The Stocks and Master Winslow

Even John, who has no great love for work, seems to have been in a great hurry to get back to the fields. So much so that he forgot his sickle and Francis had to run after him with it. Without his sickle there's no way John could harvest the Indian corn. Francis also had to lug along a scythe which is used to cut down barley and wheat. Everyone says that this fall's crop yield is about the best they've had. I'm sure Helen Billington will excuse us for leaving. We've helped her set the board back in place and goodness knows there are no dishes to be washed as each one wiped his trencher and spoon with his napkin. So let's be off.

Quite a change has taken place on the street. It's bustling with activity. Although I see some men and boys with scythes and sickles going out the palisade, others are gathered in a crowd near the west gate. Let's see what's going on, although I think I know. And how right I am! A woman and boy of about ten are sitting

In the stocks

together on a bench with their wrists and ankles thrust through a wooden board. Believe me, they're not there to rest and enjoy the afternoon sun while people stare at them. They are *set in the stocks*. This is a punishment for minor offenses. It's not an uncommon occurrence. That's why some of the onlookers are leaving to go about their business. But one is supposed to stare at the unfortunates set in the stocks because the public embarrassment is the main part of the punishment. To sit on a hard wooden bench, with your feet and hands trapped, is not exactly comfortable, but the pub-

lic shame and humiliation are what really hurt. The
boy and woman do look embarrassed and ashamed, as
you and I would, too, if we were in their place. But
they do know that they'll be set free after two hours.

One of the spectators I see is well qualified to tell us
how law and order are maintained at Plimoth. His
name is Edward Winslow. He is one of the wealthiest
men in the village, one of the most important citizens,
and the governor's chief assistant. In twentieth-century
terms he might be described as a combination secretary
of state and budget director. He is a Separatist and far
more sophisticated and better educated than most.
Though only thirty-two years old, he is never referred
to as plain Edward, nor even as Edward Winslow, but
as Master, or Mister, Winslow. This is a form of dis-
tinction which separates the richer from the poorer people, such as John.

Let's find out what Master Winslow has to say about
crime and punishment as it applies to Plimoth: "If a
man breaks the law and if accusation is brought against
him, he's heard in our meeting, open to the general."

The "general" doesn't refer to a military official, but
means that the meeting is open to the general public.
This excludes women and children (those under
twenty-one), who have no voting rights.

"At such a meeting the governor, his assistants, and
others will confer and decide whether one of the laws
that all English people recognize has been trans-
gressed."

As an example of the kind of offense which merits
someone being set in the stocks he cites the following:

"Should a woman be a common scold and rail at her husband or strangers in the street, she's like as not to be set in the stocks after a hearing."

(Just between us, I very much doubt that a man would be similarly punished for railing at his wife. Women and children are kept in their place as second-class citizens.)

The most common reason for setting a child in the stocks, he tells us, is for disobedience to a parent or to any adult. "In fact," Master Winslow says, "were a child to disobey the parent, then, according to the law, that child might be put to death, not just set in the stocks. We had one such case. But we decided that the child was mad. So it was not put to death, but set in the care of a neighbor until it was able to carry itself better."

Executing a child for serious parental disobedience is part of English common law. And the rightness of common law cannot be questioned because, as Master Winslow explains, it's strictly based upon biblical law. It does say in the Bible, for example, that a stubborn, disobedient son shall be stoned to death (Deuteronomy 21: 18–21). But I must point out that there are many other laws in the Bible which are conveniently disregarded: male circumcision and never to eat pork or shellfish, to cite just a couple. Which leads me to believe that people often use the Scripture as an excuse to justify what they want to do.

Compared to the barbaric justice carried out in England, the settlers are kind in contrast. However, Master Winslow says:

"If a child is set to watch the corn growing in the fields and he does not watch the corn and the crows come and harvest it, then many of us could starve. That is why it is a very serious offense if he fall asleep at his corn watch or walks away from it. That is why, for such disobedience, he could get more than being set in the stocks."

For this, Master Winslow says, he might be severely whipped. A public whipping post is set beside the stocks. The victim is tied to it and beaten. Worse yet, the child might even be branded with a red-hot iron. But public whippings and brandings are still a rarity here.

The ultimate punishment is death by hanging. People, including young children, are hanged for *capital crimes*. These are crimes meriting the death sentence. Under current English law there are almost two hundred such crimes listed. Most of them are crimes involving property, not crimes against people. They run the gamut from petty theft, pickpocketing, vandalism, and arson all the way to treason and, finally, murder. In England, hangings and more painful forms of execution are common events which the public looks upon as entertaining spectacles. However, the frequent executions have not reduced crime in England in the least. As a matter of fact, pickpockets attend the executions and carry on their trade while watching their fellow "craftsmen" pay the extreme penalty.

There is no gallows at Plimoth and there are no plans for erecting one. The villagers live in comparative peace and harmony. In good part, this is because Governor Bradford and his assistants do their best to keep dissatisfaction to a minimum. Poverty and starvation are not a problem here as they are in England.

But while on the subject of crime, I'm going to reveal something to you which will come as a great shock. And you must not drop a hint of it to anyone while you're here.

Remember when John Billington laughingly said that "goovnor" sometimes referred to him as "someone born to be hung"? The tragic, historical fact is that three years from now John *is* going to be "hung." Here is how Governor Bradford describes it in his history of Plimoth Plantation:

> This year [1630, in September] John Billington the elder, one that came over with the first, was arraigned, and both by grand and petty jury found guilty of wilful murder, by plain and notorious evidence. And was for the same accordingly executed. This, as it was the first execution amongst them [at Plimoth], so was it a matter of great sadness unto them. They used all due means about his trial and took the advice of Mr. Winthrop and other the ablest gentlemen in Bay of the Massachusetts, that were then newly come over, who concurred with them that he ought to die, and the land purged from blood. He and some of his had been often punished for miscarriages before, being one of the profanest families amongst them; they came from London, and I know not by what friends shuffled into their

company. His fact was that he waylaid a young man, one John Newcomen, about a former quarrel and shot him with a gun, whereof he died.*

There being no gallows in Plimoth, it was debated whether to send John back to London to be executed or to carry out the sentence here. The more immediate course was decided upon. John was hanged over the side of the fort.

Master Winslow does not see that whipping, branding, or hanging someone are contrary to Christ's teachings. When reminded that St. Matthew quotes Christ as saying ". . . that ye resist not evil: but whosoever shall smite thee on the right cheek, turn to him the other also," Master Winslow's reply is: "I am not aware that these words of Christ are contrary to our principles. If a man breaks the law, and I am sure Jesus Christ knew the scriptural law better than any man, 'tis a very serious offense. Our common law is based upon that same Scripture. Now if a man gives you a personal offense, the Christian spirit may have you turn the other cheek. Yet if he commits adultery, or murder, or he is a thief, these things are clearly against our English common law and we, as English subjects, must abide by them. Thus I see no conflict between Christ's teachings and our way of abiding by common law."

* *Of Plymouth Plantation,* by William Bradford (New York: Alfred A. Knopf, 1952), p. 234.

CHAPTER 5

Master Winslow Describes Everyday Life

Crime and punishment play a minor role in the village. So let's ask Master Winslow how he usually spends his day. Being a member of the educated, well-to-do class, and a member of the ruling class, is there a marked difference in his life-style compared to that of the majority of villagers?

One visible difference is the size of his house. It's more than twice as large as John Billington's and most of the other homes. He says that the governor allowed him to build a large house because of the size of his household. It consists of his wife, Susanna, their four children, and two servants. The house has two sleeping chambers compared to John's one. The hall is far more spacious and the loft quite a bit larger than the Billing-

Sleeping chamber

tons'. But it's a far cry from a mansion when you consider that eight people are living in what adds up to little more than three rooms.

Despite his social position, Master Winslow says that he works in the fields, just like everyone else, during planting and harvesting seasons.

" 'Twas new to me, as I'm not from a shire in England where farming is the main endeavor. So 'twas new to me. Yet there's not that much one has to learn and there are none of us who can afford not to help at time of planting and at harvest."

During the winter months, when outdoor chores are limited to gathering firewood and mending fences and buildings, Master Winslow spends a good part of his time taking care of the plantation's business affairs. This includes corresponding with the merchant adventurers and other business people in England. And now that Plimoth is independent from the English investors, he is one of the key men responsible for increasing the beaver trade with the Indians. Beaver pelts are very much in demand in England and bring a good price. This is helping the villagers to eventually meet their annual payments to the merchant adventurers.

Here is how Master Winslow describes his average day: "Exactly what I do during the day dependeth on the season. But in my own case, in the morning I'm lying abed thinking about getting up. And how long I think about getting up dependeth upon what's to be done. I'll hear one of my boys browsing about outside looking for the chickens so that he can gather eggs. And I'll hear my wife poking about the house, too. On Sundays, though, she'll lie abed a bit longer. Because she's forbidden to work upon the Sabbath, 'tis a cold meal we'll have on Sunday."

Especially during the winter months, he sometimes spends his afternoons visiting from house to house. "Aside from the gossiping, there might be recreations to the manner of telling tales and recollections of events and adventures in the Old World. And sometimes we play outdoors at *stool ball* or *hoop rolling*. Because we're Englishmen, we do like to talk, and there's much

Playing stool ball

sitting about and talking. Then, before you know, it's time for the small meal, about six of the clock, and thence to bed."

But daily life is far from leisurely. Aside from the agricultural pursuits and tending to the livestock, meats and fish have to be preserved, fruits and vegetables dried or pickled. Grains, such as barley and wheat, have to be threshed and stored in sacks or barrels. Butter and cheese, and let's not forget beer, have to be made. In addition, there's the constant need to repair roofs, chimneys, and floors, as well as new buildings to erect.

Hoop rolling

However, compared to the kind of life their grand-children and great-grandchildren will face, the Plimoth villagers are leading a life of leisure. For New Englanders, both before and after the American Revolution, will work twelve to fourteen hours a day, six and sometimes even seven days a week, and all year round. There will be practically no such thing as free time. Why does this increase in the workload come about? Certainly the Plimouth people aren't lazy. Rather, the future colonists will have to be far more self-sufficient than the first settlers. With the exception of most of their food and buildings, everything the Plimoth villagers need comes from England. And the list is large: clothing, sheets, blankets, bedding, shoes, boots, cooking utensils, tools, even furniture. No one owns a spinning wheel to spin yarn, let alone a loom to weave cloth. There's no blacksmith, at present, to forge and fashion andirons, axheads, and other needed iron tools. There's no tinsmith to make cooking utensils and oil lamps. There's no potter to make drinking mugs, bowls, or trenchers. In short, aside from a few carpenters and two coopers who make barrels, there are no local craftsmen.

Because all the cloth and clothing is imported from England, the women don't have to spend the long hours it takes to spin wool into yarn and flax into linen. And they're spared the time-consuming labor of weaving yarn into cloth. The men, too, are spared the long hours and hard work required to raise and shear sheep and then process the wool so it can be spun. Nor do they face all the work it takes to plant, harvest, and process

Cooper making a barrel

Harvesting

flax to be spun into linen. It is these kinds of tasks that would take up so much of the latter-day colonists' time so that they could be independent of England.

However, the villagers pay a steep price for being spared this kind of work. Most of them own very little clothing, sometimes to the point of discomfort, including having to go barefoot at times. Furniture and other household comforts, as you've seen, are at a minimum. To make their situation worse, money is scarce. Yet they have to buy all their necessities from English merchants in London who charge them as much as they can.

However, most of the villagers were used to having just the bare necessities before they came over. Consequently, they probably don't feel in the least underprivileged. Above all, they realize that their future prospects in Plimoth are much more promising than if they had remained in Holland or England. Their hopes for a better way of life have already been fulfilled. Most of them now own their homes and a good parcel of land.

By the way, we never did go outside the palisade to watch the men harvesting. However, as John Billington would say: "It 'tain't sooch an fascinatin' thing to obsarve." So, instead, let's go to the meetinghouse and see what we can learn.

CHAPTER 6

Sunday Service and the Separatist Faith

The meetinghouse is directly underneath the fort's gun deck. Aside from being used for town meetings, the large room is used for church services on Sundays. Because religion plays such an important role in everyone's life here, let me tell you something about it.

Notice that the meeting room doesn't have the kinds of decorations you might expect to see in a church. The Separatists don't believe in fancy adornments. Statues of saints and stained glass windows, to their way of thinking, are sinful to display. The room is purely functional. The stark, backless wooden benches aren't the ultimate in comfort. There's no fireplace to heat the room during the cold weather. However, this is not because the worshipers prefer to shiver during town meeting or while attending Sunday services. The main reason is that the gun deck is directly overhead and gunpowder has to be stored in the building. Besides, no one is used to much in the way of warm room temperatures, as you've already seen.

The Separatists' religious beliefs are rooted in the Puritan faith. They believe that everyone is born with a strong tendency to be bad. Worse yet, there's nothing one can do about this. Only God can. He alone determines whether one is to be evil or good. Therefore, the better one's relation to Him is, the better one's chances are for being good. Furthermore, the Separatists believe that our future has already been determined from the day we are born. Some people are destined for eternal damnation, the more fortunate for ultimate salvation. Here again, God is the one who decides this.

Offhand this seems like a helpless, depressing kind of outlook. But not so for the Separatists, because they hopefully believe that God has selected them to be among the saved. This does appear to leave the majority of people here in Plimoth, the Anglicans, to face an unhappy future. But it's not hopeless for them—they can save themselves by switching to the Separatists' religion. Conversion is made quite easy. There's no long trial period, but the would-be convert must pass a test to make sure that his faith is genuine.

On the other hand, if a Church member behaves badly, he is ejected from the Church—excommunicated. A person may be excommunicated for drunkenness, swearing, blasphemy, or immoral acts of any kind. But one is not doomed thereby to permanent damnation. For when he sees the error of his ways and the congregation feels that he is sincerely repentant, he is welcomed back into the sect of the saved.

The Separatist Church is governed simply and democratically. The *pastor,* who's elected by the congregation, is the head of the Church. He conducts the Sunday service, baptizes, and offers communion. Next in line is the *teaching elder,* who acts as an assistant pastor. Where there is no pastor, as is the case here in Plimoth, he is in full charge. An elder, however, is not allowed to perform baptisms or offer communion. Lastly, there are *deacons* and *deaconesses.* The deacons collect money from the congregation, pay the pastor, and distribute alms to the poor and sick. A deaconess' responsibility is to call on the poor and sick people. She is a kind of visiting nurse and social worker. She also has to keep the children from misbehaving during church service.

A woman's place in the Church is on a par with her position in the home and in the community: second-class. During service she's not allowed to utter a word other than to sing Psalms and pray. She's not allowed to vote in Church elections.

The Separatists are much stricter about following what is set forth in the Bible than the Anglicans, though not as strict as the Puritans. They forbid any ceremony to be included in church services that doesn't conform to what's in the Scripture. For example, their clergymen are not allowed to dress in fancy robes. They wear the same clothing as everyone else. No hymns are sung since there are no hymns in the Bible. Psalms are sung instead. Neither marriages nor burials are accompanied with a church ceremony. They are strictly lay affairs. There is no confirmation ceremony for this too has no scriptural precedent. I might add that women are looked upon as inferior to men because this, too, has its basis in the Scripture. For it states in Genesis that God made Adam first, in His own image. Eve came as an afterthought to serve as Adam's helper. And instead of being made in God's image, she was fashioned from one of Adam's ribs. This belief in woman's origin helped to establish her secondary rank.

Since you won't be staying long enough to attend a Sunday service, I'll describe it to you. I don't think you'll regret missing the experience because Sunday service begins at eight in the morning and lasts until noon. But that's not the end. It resumes around two and continues until five or six o'clock.

It undoubtedly must seem strange to you that men, women, and especially children spend an entire Sunday in church. The fact is that there's not much else one can or may do on the Sabbath. A little while ago Master Winslow told us that his wife was not allowed to cook on Sundays. In fact, any form of work is forbidden. This is based upon the Scripture which states that the seventh day is a day of rest. It is also a religious day, and therefore games, sports, and socializing are not the way to pass the time. Since religion plays such a vital role, it makes sense to the Separatists for people to devote one day a week to it so they can learn more and more about their faith.

Master William Brewster serves as a combination teaching and ruling elder. He conducts the services and is in complete charge of Church affairs. Not too long ago he wrote to Pastor William Robinson in Leyden, who had been the Separatists' pastor when they were living in Holland. Elder Brewster asked him to appoint him as pastor for the Plimoth church. But his request was refused. Pastor Robinson stated that one had to have a university degree to qualify for such a position. In a way, this seems to me to be a rather arbitrary decision. Elder Brewster had attended Cambridge University, though he did not stay long enough to complete his degree. Furthermore, he was one of the original founders of the Separatist sect in England twenty years before. Pastor Robinson's ruling, however, has not posed any serious drawbacks for Elder Brewster. Other than not being able to perform baptisms or offer communion, he appears to run the church to everyone's satisfaction.

It is common custom for pastors to offer lengthy prayers which drone on for hours. Elder Brewster believes in short and frequent ones instead. This, he thinks, makes it less likely that some members of the congregation will fall asleep.

Aside from the frequent prayers, how are the seven or eight hours of churching passed? Many Psalms are sung. But a good deal of the time is passed in what is called *prophesying*. It has nothing to do with foretelling the future. A leading member of the congregation reads a passage from the Bible. Then he explains at length what he thinks it means. Sometimes the elder adds to what the prophesier has said, or he may even offer a different interpretation. This practice uses up a good deal of time. Its purpose is to involve everyone in the

At Sunday service

meaning of the Scripture and to help them understand
its relevance to everyday conduct.

Between sermon after sermon, Psalm singing, and
prophesying the time does pass—at least, as far as the
grown-ups are concerned; in fact, it's their only intellec-
tual entertainment. However, it must be a bit trying for
the children to sit for hours on end listening to mostly in-
comprehensible talk. But, as you know, children in 1627
are used to doing as they're told.

Interestingly enough, the majority of the people attending service are not Separatists but Anglicans. Some of them probably are not thrilled by the form and length of Sunday service. And the presence of the Strangers, as the Separatists call them, is occasionally embarassing to the Separatists. But English law makes it compulsory for everyone to go to church. And since the governor is a strict upholder of the law, there's no alternative because there's no other building to hold services in.

You and I have been sitting on this hard bench for less than fifteen minutes. Imagine if we had to stay seated for hours more. But since we don't have to, let's leave and do some more exploring, in the fort and down the street.

CHAPTER 7

The Fort,
Miles Standish,
and Indians

Now that we've examined the room inside the fort let's explore the gun deck on top. To get to it we have to climb this ladder, so follow me carefully, one rung at a time. I'm sure that the first thing that's caught your attention up here are the six cannons which ring the gun deck. They're called *pieces* and were brought over from England. The large ones are called *sakers*. They fire an iron ball that weighs almost five pounds. The smaller pieces are called *minions*. Each of them weighs over twelve hundred pounds. Imagine the amount of manpower it took to mount them up here with nothing more than block and tackle. No cranes or derricks.

Captain Miles Standish, who is in charge of Plimoth's defenses, is the only settler with any kind of mili-

Gun deck and cannon

tary training. He explained to me that when he was a young man he had served in Queen Elizabeth's army.

"I was sent to the Low Countries to fight with the Dutch against the French. In Holland I encountered Master William Brewster and he persuaded me to come over. My duties, he told me, would be to train up the men and the handling of the great pieces."

When fired, these "great pieces" make a terrific noise and belch forth huge puffs of smoke and flame. The captain has assured me that it's not "sound and fury signifying nothing." He claims that a skilled gunner, by which he probably means himself, can aim a saker with such accuracy that he can hit a ship half a mile away down there in the bay, though up to now, he's never had to put this to the test. He does, however, drill his militiamen regularly once or twice a day. The militia is made up of all the men in the town, who take turns being on active duty. He teaches them how to march in formation and to fire their muskets on command. The settlers also have a sentry manning the gun deck twenty-four hours a day.

Why the settlers need a sentry and engage in so much drilling is a bit mystifying. They live in peaceful rela-

Militiamen firing muskets

tions with the Indians. The sole danger that might occur would be the arrival of a French or Spanish or pirate ship in the harbor below. But this would seem an unlikely event. When I asked Captain Standish what exactly his militiamen had to guard against, he said somewhat defensively: "On our earliest explorations, before we settled to build on this Cap of Cod, we encountered Indians. They shot at us with their odd, long bows and we replied with musket fire. There ware none killed on either side, but I can say straight away that my militia stand ready at all times. They serve a constant watch over the plantation."

Captain Standish, by the way, is not a Separatist. Like the majority of the *Mayflower* passengers, he came over with his wife, Rose, in the hope of improving their living conditions. He seems to think it was indeed a good choice. He told me: "There ware many of us who will settle without the palisade and farm upon our own. I've three sons, John, Charles, and Alexander, and we'll settle up to the northward of here and I'll name it Duxbarrow after an area of my family what hath lived in Lancashire."

He never would have had such an opportunity to own land if he had remained back in England. Unfortunately, however, his wife, Rose, died during that first awful winter. His present wife and the mother of his sons is named Barbara.

"I met Barbara when she ware quite small girl. Her ware the younger sister of Rose. I did take notice of her in a dance. Her did a fine, sprightly turn and I sent for her when Rose died."

Although the captain is not a Separatist, he is a key member of Governor Bradford's inner council. He's also one of the men who has been given the responsibility for furthering the beaver trade with the Indians. The sale of beaver fur to the English is the settlers' main source of income. Captain Standish not only has learned to speak a bit of Wapanoagian (a neighboring Indian tribe's language), but is on very friendly terms with Hobomok who is a Wampanoag. Hobomok sometimes stays at Captain Standish's house. Another Indian who often stayed here, a friend of the governor's, was Squanto. He died five years ago. The captain was not overly fond of him and said to me: "I trusted Squanto not overmuch, myself, for he was not always fair with his own people. If they trusted him not, how could we?"

But the captain added that Squanto was most important to the settlers since he spoke excellent English and that it was Squanto who originally taught the settlers how to plant and raise Indian corn. That is the chief crop grown here and you know it as corn. Above all, Squanto helped them expand their beaver trade with the other Indian tribes.

How the settlers met their first Indian is quite a fascinating story. Early in March of 1621 a meeting was being held in the common house. This was just after that first, terrible winter during which so many had died. As a result, the settlers were not yet well enough organized to guard their partially built village. Consequently, an Indian succeeded in walking into the compound, down the main path, now the main street, and proceeded toward the common house without being challenged. To say the least, the people were surprised to see an Indian suddenly appear. His greeting astounded them even more: "Welcome, Englishmen," he said.

The Indian was clothed in nothing more than a leather string around his waist with a bit of fringe dangling in front. Some of the men immediately draped a red horseman's coat around him. (They were more embarrassed by his nakedness than concerned about keeping him warm.) He told them that his name was Samoset and hinted that he enjoyed beer. Having none, they served him "strong water," which is what they sometimes call hard liquor. They then plied him with food and asked him endless questions. It was the first time they had met an Indian.

He told them that he was chief of a subtribe of the Abnaki, who lived in Maine. He had learned English from the sailors who fished off the Maine coast, which is undoubtedly how he learned to like beer as well. He informed the Plimoth settlers that the site they were occupying was actually land belonging to the Patuxet Indians. However, the entire tribe had been wiped out by a plague a few years previous. This terrible sickness was probably smallpox. It is upsetting for us to realize that Europeans not only succeeded in conquering and wiping out most of the Indians on this continent through force of arms, but also introduced them to some additional "blessings" of the white man's culture: smallpox and tuberculosis. These diseases killed off countless Indians over the years.

But to continue, Samoset returned a few days later accompanied by Squanto, the only surviving Patuxet. He had been taken to England in 1605 by an English explorer, Captain George Weymouth, and remained there for nine years. During that time he learned fluent English. Because of this, Captain John Smith had him sail with him in 1614 to the New World to help in dealing and trading with the Indians. When Captain Smith sailed back to England, he left a Captain Hunt in charge of the trading post. He was to load his ship with fish and beaver skins and then return to England. Instead, Hunt engaged in what he thought would be a far more profitable venture. He kidnaped twenty Patuxets, including Squanto, and seven Nauset Indians. Hunt then sailed to Spain and sold the "salvages" in the slave market at Malaga. Somehow, Squanto survived this frightful situation and succeeded in getting to England. There he lived with a wealthy merchant for several years. Eight years ago, in 1619, he returned to his native land with another English captain. He discovered the tragic fate of his tribe and settled with the Wampanoag Indians and became a friend of Hobomok.

I regret to have to mention that, though the settlers' relationship with the Indians is peaceful now, as time goes on this will change. When more and more colonists settle here and to the north, the situation will become worse. The Indians will have their land forcibly taken away and be mercilessly exploited and often massacred.

CHAPTER 8

Indentured Servants and Goodman Dotey

It's now close to five of the clock, as they say in Plimoth. Many of the men are on their way home from the fields. If I'm not mistaken, the man just ahead of us, carrying a large bundle of harvested Indian corn, is Edward Dotey. I'm most anxious for you to meet him, because until just recently he was an *indentured servant*.

Before we talk to him, let me tell you what it means to be an indentured servant. Eighteen of them came over on the *Mayflower*. That's a large proportion of servants to masters, considering that most of the other eighty-four passengers were poor people. Who, then, could afford a servant? Anyone who could manage to pay for his or her passage, which wasn't very much. In exchange, the person whose passage was paid agreed to work as a servant for a period of time, in order to repay his or her debt. There's nothing unusual about this kind of arrangement. Indentured servitude is common in England. Poor parents often hire out one or more of their children to another family. The child must serve the master for a specified length of time, usually seven years. This arrangement saves the parents the expense of feeding and clothing the child. The master must assume these responsibilities. Some parents place their children out for indenture because they think it is good training for a child to live with and work for someone else. This may seem like quite a heartless way to treat a little one. But remember that children are not considered special, delicate creatures, but as miniature adults and therefore they must share the burdens of existence.

What's it like for a child, or an adult, to be an indentured servant? To start with, he loses what few personal rights he may have had. He must be respectful to his master and to his master's family. Above all, he must be as obedient as a dog and do anything he is ordered to do. He has no time of his own. His twenty-four hours a day belong to his master. He has no right to time off unless the master lets him have a few hours for play or leisure. There are no holidays except Sundays, when he can do his resting and relaxing in compulsory church attendance.

Because of the limited housing space, the indentured servant lives on an intimate basis with master and family. He eats with them, shares sleeping quarters with them, and works alongside the others. But he is not looked upon as an equal. He is definitely considered an inferior and is expected to consider himself as such.

Those are some of the disadvantages. But there are

At work in Plimoth

compensations. An indentured servant knows that he will be fed, clothed, and have a place to sleep. It's the master's responsibility to provide him with these basic necessities. Many poor people in England have to beg or steal to keep alive. When you consider that alternative, indenture is not all that bad.

How well a master clothes and feeds his servant is another matter. However, here at Plimoth, if it becomes obvious that a master is starving or mistreating his servant, the servant can call the situation to the attention of the governor. He, in turn, can summon the master to attend a hearing, in order to determine whether the complaint is justified. Up to now, I'm given to understand, no master has been brought to trial for such abuse. Indentured servants are becoming somewhat scarce because many are reaching the end of their service contracts and becoming freemen. Thus it makes sense not to maltreat them.

Unfortunately, in future decades, when servants become less of a scarce commodity, there will be instances of shameful maltreatment. I know of one frightful example involving a thirteen-year-old boy in Plimoth. He was found dead under suspicious circumstances. The cause of his death was immediately looked into. To everyone's horror, it was discovered that his master, a Robert Latham, not only overworked him and underfed him, but beat him so severely that he died. The court did take rather severe measures: the master was sentence to be "burned in the hand" (branded) and all his property was taken away.

Another, though far less gruesome, instance of an unhappy result of child indenture happened only a few years hence. It involved none other than John Billington's son, Francis, whom you've met. Francis and his wife, Christiana, indentured their five-year-old son, Joseph. Poor little Joseph was so miserable, being away from home and obviously not very kindly treated by his master, that he ran away and returned to his parents several times. The master made a complaint to the court, feeling that he was being cheated. The court de-

cided that Joseph was a bit too young to be punished—
he could have been publicly whipped or even branded
for such disobedience. Instead, the court sentenced
Francis and his wife to be set in the stocks for each
time they allowed their son to stay with them. Although
Joseph did escape immediate punishment, he was, it
seems to me, sentenced to years of unhappiness.

Being an indentured servant does seem like slavery.
But, in actual fact, there are important differences. A
slave remains a slave for life unless his master chooses
to set him free. An indentured servant's time of servitude is usually limited to a maximum of seven years.
Furthermore, it is not unusual for masters to give the
newly freed servant gifts of money, clothing, or even
bushels of corn to help him get a start. It differs from
slavery in still another way. An indentured servant's
body is not considered his master's property, only his
time of servitude. Therefore he cannot be sold outright
like a slave to another master. For example, if a servant
has three more years to serve, his service time can be
sold to someone else, but at the end of three years he
must automatically be given his freedom. Sad to relate,
in a few years from now, both Indians and blacks will
be forced into indentured servitude but these rights will
not apply. They will be looked upon as pieces of property that can be sold to someone else with no limit to
time of servitude. This is outright slavery no matter
what it's called.

Now that you know about some of the grim realities
of indentured servitude, let's learn about it at first hand
from Edward Dotey. He is a man of twenty-eight who

has a very modest opinion of his position in the community. He makes it clear that, under no circumstances, should he be addressed as "Master Dotey."

" 'Master,' " he says, "is an title of respect which I don't really own. Instead, thou may address me as 'Goodman Dotey.' 'Goodman' means that I am both a Christian man and yeoman farmer, but not of great wealth."

Goodman Dotey is not a Separatist. Why then did he indenture himself in order to come to the New World?

"As a youth I did live in Essex, bein' some two days journey north of London Town. One day my father said to me, 'Edward, you're not the first-born so you'll get none of my land. So you ought endenture thyself to a man what hath land.' So I did journey into London Town. And there I doth work for some years doin' lowly tasks such as unloadin' ships, sail mendin', and such like. I did decide ne'er to take up any special trade to become such thing as a tailor, carpenter, smith, or the like. While in London Town I met with Stephen Hopkins who did tell me he was comin' to the New World. He said, 'If you come and work for me, you shall receive land and there's great land there and a chance at great advancement.' I did always wish to be a farmer and so I did come over on the *Mayflower* with him."

Stephen Hopkins paid for Edward Dotey's passage in return for which Dotey agreed to work for him for seven years to pay off the debt. He knew that during that time he would be provided with clothing, all his meals, and a place to sleep. His contract with Master

Hopkins ended a little over a month ago and he is now a freeman and a full-fledged citizen of Plimoth Plantation. As such, he recently received one share in Plimoth's property. This is a remarkable change in status. From being an indentured servant who owned nothing, not even his own time, he is now a landowner with twenty-one acres to plant, harvest, and build on.

Here is how he describes a typical day now that he is a freeman: "I am a single man, and as a single man, I would not be havin' my own household. For if I go off to the fields, who should cook and who should tend the house? So I do still live with the Hopkinses. Bein' a single man in his household and gettin' room and board, I do work for Master Hopkins, as well as work my own land."

However, he quickly adds. "When there is a single woman in the colony what does appeal to me, I shall certainly attempt to be married. Then I will build my own house on my land which lies to the north, outside the palisade."

There were very few single women here in the early years, but their number has been increasing. Some of the nine ships that have come from England since 1620 have brought over the wives and children of men who came across on the *Mayflower*. After the latter made certain that they could earn a living in this new country, they sent for their families. These often included daughters and other female relatives, some of whom are now of marriageable age.

"Then too," Goodman Dotey says, "other single women come over here knowin' that there are twenty

Plimoth women

single men what would be married. 'Tis good advancement for a young lady to marry a man what owns land, for 'tis a promise for the future. Such single women first attach themselves to a household."

Goodman Dotey's experience, from indentured servant to freeman and landowner, is not exceptional. As time goes on, more and more such servants will become freemen. On the other hand, there will be, and probably are now, other indentured servants whose futures may not be improved.

There is another side to everyday life in Plimoth which is as important here as it is in your time: medical care. What happens when someone is sick or has injured himself? Let's visit with Mr. Samuel Fuller, who is supposed to be an expert on the subject.

CHAPTER 9

"Bad Medicine" and Deacon Fuller

We're on our way to Samuel Fuller's house. He serves the plantation as physician and surgeon because he is considered a learned man who has read some medical books and had, in the past, worked with the ship's surgeon on the voyage over on the *Mayflower*. His seven years' "practice" in Plimoth, it is hoped, have added to his knowledge.

While we're on our way I'll describe what medical care is like in this day and age in the Western World. And believe me, it's unlike anything you might imagine. For *physiology* (how the body functions) and *anatomy* (how the body is structured) are not based on scientific study. Instead, medical practice is tangled up in religious beliefs, superstitions, and assumptions which go back two thousand years to ancient Greece. And practically no progress has been made in all that stretch of time. Changes, yes, but progress, no.

When you cut yourself, you know that you should use an antiseptic to prevent infection. If it is a severe cut, a doctor stops the bleeding, disinfects the wound, stitches it together, and applies a sterile bandage. He may even give you an antibiotic to make certain that no infection will ensue. When someone becomes seriously ill in the last quarter of the twentieth century, there's often a drug or an operation that will cure the ailment. Though this is not always the case, it is a comparatively safe assumption. Operations are painless, thanks to anesthesia, and usually not fatal. It's also taken for granted that childbirth is now a comparatively painless procedure for the mother and safe for both mother and infant. The infant mortality rate in the United States in the 1970s is about 16.1 deaths per thousand live births. The infant mortality rate here at Plimoth in 1627 is at least ten times greater.

The advances in modern medicine will not start taking place in Europe until the mid-nineteenth century. Prior to that time there will be very little change from the methods used in Plimoth and throughout the Western World.

The plantation in 1627 has no surgeon or physician. Samuel Fuller is the nearest to one the settlers have, although he has no professional training. However, this is probably not at all a disadvantage, for the way medical professionals practice their supposed skills these days is far more apt to bring about death than a cure.

James I, King of England until two years ago, seemed to have been well aware of this. For, though he was sickly throughout his life, he never permitted a

Woodcut by Hans Holbein the Younger:
"Death and the Physician"

physician to take care of him. To show you what he escaped and what medical care can be like, this is how
doctors will try to save the life of Charles II, his grand-
son. The king will have a stroke and become uncon-
scious. The first thing the royal physicians will do is to
take a pint of blood from a vein in his arm. They will
cut into his shoulder and withdraw eight more ounces
of blood. This is just the beginning. He will be given
drugs to make his bowels move, plus an enema. The
enema contained all kinds of strange things: violets,
fennel seed, linseed, cinnamon, and saffron. In addition,

they will shave his head and raise a blister on his scalp. He will be forced to take sneezing powder "to strengthen his brain." Wine, mixed with an extract of thistle leaves, will be poured down his throat. To complete the cure the great physicians will place a paste of pigeon dung and pitch on his feet. Understandably, the poor king's condition will not improve. As a final remedy—the last in their hideous bag of tricks—the doctors will force forty drops of human skull extract down his throat. Then the unfortunate monarch will die.

Much of such medical nonsense is the result of the teachings of Galen, a second-century Greek physician. He maintained that the human body consists of four humors. They are choler (hot and dry), phlegm (cold and moist), sanguine (hot and moist), and melancholy (cold and dry). Sickness occurs when one of these humors gets out of balance. For instance, if there is too much heat, a cooling drug should be applied. If there is an excess of wetness, one lets out blood from the body.

Galen's knowledge of human antomy was practically nil. And for thirteen hundred years afterward almost nothing more was learned. One of the reasons for this continuing ignorance was that the Catholic Church forbade anyone to dissect a human body in order to learn how it was constructed. Until less than one hundred years ago, just about everyone "knew" for a fact that males were missing one rib because God used it to make Eve. There are probably people here at Plimoth who still believe this.

However, in the 1540s, Andreas Vesalius, an Italian, was allowed to "make an anatomy" on executed crimi-

Dissecting a corpse

nals. He exposed the myth of the missing rib. He also discovered a number of errors in Galen's medical theories. But he was careful about not exposing too many. Understandably so, because a contemporary, Michael Servetus, was sentenced by the Church to be burned at the stake for exposing one of Galen's faulty claims. The Church, you see, held Galen in high esteem. And what the Church upheld, no man should challenge.

Another man who has had a strong influence on to-day's medical practice was Paracelsus. He lived during the early part of the sixteenth century. Among other things, he experimented with chemicals as cures for illnesses. Some of his findings may have been a slight improvement over Galen's. But he combined astrology with his theories, which didn't add much to their scientific soundness. When we talk to Samuel Fuller, I think you'll notice his influence.

With this kind of background influencing the practice of medicine, what do the people here at Plimoth face when they're sick or injured?

Wounds: Severe cuts, from wielding scythes, sickles, knives and axes are not uncommon. How are such injuries treated? Until about fifty years ago, boiling oil was poured immediately into the wound. Then it was bound up with any kind of cloth at hand, clean or not. Fortunately, Ambroise Paré, a French surgeon, changed this cruel and useless procedure.

Paré started his surgical training as a barber's apprentice in 1529. Then, while still a young man, he became a surgeon in the French army. Instead of using the boiling-oil treatment on wounded soldiers, he tried something else. He applied a salve of egg yolks and oil of roses to the wound, stitched it together, and used a drain to rid it of pus. Much to his relief, for he wasn't certain at first, he found that many more wounded men survived with his method. Thanks to him, wounds are now treated similarly. Although it's a far cry from twentieth-century antiseptic methods, it's not completely useless.

Surgery: The only kind of operation that might be performed at Plimoth is amputation. It would only be done as a last resort, for it can mean the last of the patient. There's no anesthesia, no knowledge of how to stop profuse bleeding, and no awareness of the need for utmost cleanliness. Even the surgeons in England don't attempt an abdominal operation. They realize that it would be fatal in all instances. Consequently, anyone here who has an attack of appendicitis or any other serious internal problem is more often than not doomed to die.

Diseases and plagues: Influenza, or flu, is probably one of the few communicable diseases you know of, though you call it something else. It's a sickness that is transmitted from one person to another and often spreads from one community to another. However, a late twentieth-century flu epidemic will seem almost trifling compared to the kinds of epidemics that can occur here in 1627 in Plimoth.

Here, everyone faces the danger of catching fatal diseases which you probably never even heard of. They are: diphtheria, typhoid fever, cholera, smallpox, and, worst of all, the bubonic plague. In 1625, only two years ago, Londoners suffered from a severe epidemic. Sometimes called the "black plague," or just the "plague," in England, it spreads like wildfire in populated towns where unsanitary conditions are at their worst. In large towns, such as London, rats are as common as mosquitoes in a swampy region. They are the

London during a plague

chief carriers of the plague, because fleas, which infest these rodents, transmit the diseases to humans. Because personal cleanliness is practically nonexistent, fleas enjoy an unrestricted human hunting ground.

It is estimated that, in the fourteenth century, 25 million people in Europe alone—over one fourth of the population—died of the plague. The death toll in London, two years ago, was frightful. To date, Plimoth has escaped this horror. Most probably because it is not a crowded community, is comparatively clean, and is thousands of miles from England.

Smallpox is another common, contagious disease. It was introduced to the New World in the sixteenth century by the Spaniards when they invaded Mexico. Three and one-half million people, mainly Indians, died from it. It spread northward and, as you know, wiped out an entire Indian tribe right here. I might add that in six years—in 1633—it will kill off a number of people here, including Samuel Fuller.

Women and childbirth: Women are the main victims of these dark ages of medical science in Europe. It is they who bear children and so bear the brunt of this woeful ignorance.

At delivery time, a mother is attended by a midwife. Samuel Fuller's wife, Bridgett, is the midwife here in Plimoth. Under normal conditions, such assistance allows the mother to give birth, usually successfully, but when complications arise, which is not uncommon, the results are often fatal to both mother and baby.

In England at this time, there are two Chamberlen brothers, both (oddly) named Peter, who have invented the obstetrical forceps. This surgical tool, still used in the twentieth century, has helped make childbirth less painful and dangerous. But the Chamberlens refuse to allow anyone else to use or copy their invention, so that they can make all the money from the high fees they charge their patients. Denied this help, mothers at Plimoth, as well as elsewhere, face needless risk and suffering.

Mother and infant everywhere now face still another danger: childbed fever. It can result from dirty, unwashed hands of the midwife or doctor tending the delivery and usually causes fatal infection. Childbed fever will continue to cause the death of millions of women in Europe for more than two hundred years.

Drugs: Aside from herbs and flowers, the weirdest kinds of drugs are used in Europe at this time. The most recommended one to counteract poison is *powdered unicorn horn.* As we know today, there is no such animal as a unicorn. The apothecaries (druggists) and physicians in 1627 probably know this too. They grind up elephant tusks or any other animal's horn into a powder and no one knows the difference.

The *bezoar stone* is still another drug used for many kinds of illnesses. It's only available to the rich as it's expensive. But this is small loss to the poor people as it is nothing more or less than a gallstone.

One of the strangest medications is called *usnea*. It comes from moss scraped from the skull of a criminal who has been hung in chains for a long while. Second best to this horrid and useless remedy are bits of cut-up hangman's rope. Executioners in England sell this gruesome product to the highest bidder after hangings.

With such medical ignorance the order of the day, it's hard to imagine how people manage to remain alive at all. But obviously they do. However, the average life expectancy in 1627 is twenty years. In our twentieth century it's sixty-nine in the U.S. The reason life expectancy is so low in 1627 is because so many deaths occur during infancy and childhood. This pulls the average down. Once past those dangerous years, a person's chances for longevity are quite good.

Our friends in Plimoth are, on the whole, far healthier than Londoners. Men who live to age twenty-one can expect to live until they're sixty-nine; women, to sixty-two. Men and women who live until thirty can expect to live until they're seventy and sixty-five, respectively.

As you can see, women have a shorter life expectancy. And when one compares the death rate of men to women, the high price women pay for childbearing becomes starkly apparent. Between ages twenty-two to twenty-nine, less than 1 per cent of men die (0.6 per cent)—for women, the death rate is almost ten times greater (5.9 per cent). Between ages thirty to thirty-nine, the women's death rate is four times greater than the men's (12 per cent versus 3.6 per cent).

Now let's find out what Samuel Fuller has to say about medical care. A man in his late forties, he is usually addressed as "Deacon Fuller" because he's a deacon of the church. He's a man of means, and his home is among the larger ones, comparable to Master Winslow's.

Deacon Fuller frankly admits that he has had no medical training. He says that physicians in England take, as he puts it, "a great course of study at a university." You and I know, however, that his lack of professional training is scarcely a handicap.

"I have got some skill at surgery," he says, "for I do know the secrets of anatomy—where the joints do join and the veins do lie for to let blood. As well, I can perform extraction of teeth and purging with physic."

Although Deacon Fuller hints that he has performed amputations, I frankly doubt it. On the other hand, I have little doubt that he could perform an amputation just as well as the professional butchers in England.

Naturally, Fuller is a great believer in bloodletting. This is how he describes one way it is done: "You take a cup and make it hot, place it quickly over some part where you have made a slice and put it there and it will make a suction and draw blood."

He is emphatic about the dangers that can result from washing one's body: "It can be found that the most noxious vapors and infections are spirits that engender themselves in winds and waters. So it is very dangerous to one's health to scrub your skin with water or to ever expose it to the wind. And so we avoid it whenever we can. The only time you will use any bath whatsoever is as medicine as to bathe with rose water for its particular virtues."

Illnesses for which there are no cures, pain for which there is no relief, childbirth accompanied with frequent deaths are accepted as the price one must pay for being human. But the settlers face such calamities with calm resignation because, for better or for worse, they believe they are God's will. In the twentieth century, people rely on science to cure all human miseries which, unfortunately, it does not always do.

Deacon Fuller expresses the attitude of his Plimoth people as follows: "God is to be praised by those who live through illness and for those what dieth. For God taketh some where he wisheth them to go and is to be praised for that. And those he taketh are not lamented. And for those that live—that, too, is the Lord's purpose and for that he is to be praised. The Lord giveth and the Lord taketh according to his will."

Tomorrow, your last day here, we'll have the chance

to be part of a far happier side of life. We're going to learn about a wedding celebration that lasts all day. So now let's go back to the Billington house, have supper, and get a good night's sleep. And please don't stare at John Billington because of what you know about his future.

CHAPTER 10

Mary Bartlet and Her Wedding Day

Up to now, we've talked to a number of Plimoth men to get their points of view. But we've not talked to any women to find out how they feel about life here. So, today, I've arranged for us to visit with Mary Warren Bartlet, a young woman who was married the day before you arrived.

At present, Mary and her husband, Robert, are living with her parents, the Warrens. Their house is the second to last one at the end of the street, toward seaside. It's one of the bigger homes and certainly needs to be because the Warren family is the largest in the village. There's Richard, the father, his wife, Elizabeth, and seven children. They range in age from less than one year old to Mary, who's twenty. In addition, an indentured servant, a boy in his early teens, lives with them. With Mary's husband staying there as well, living conditions are crowded, to say the least. However,

View of the sea and the Warrens' house

Mary and Robert plan to build a house of their own next spring, on his twenty-one acres outside the palisade.

What with children scampering, crawling, and clamoring about, added to all the household chores that must be done for so large a family, Mary agreed with me that there'd be more confusion than conversation if we visited with her at home. So we're meeting at a favorite spot of hers just outside the palisade. It overlooks the ocean. The distant sound of the great waves breaking on the shore is like a muffled lullaby offset by the raucous caws of the herring gulls.

Mary is already waiting for us. She's so slight and young looking she seems more like a girl in her mid-teens than a bride of twenty. It's difficult to picture her twenty-five years from now when she'll be in her mid-forties. And in all likelihood, like her mother, she'll have given birth to almost a dozen children, eight or nine of them surviving, and the most recent one less than a year old.

Mary doesn't look upon such a childbearing future with either fear or resentment. Probably quite the contrary. For she believes that it's woman's purpose to bear children constantly, nurture them, and tend to the home. Mary says she has had excellent training for her new role: "I been helpin' me mother with all that for years now, havin' many little ones to take care of, we bein' a family of nine folks."

It would never occur to her that it's unfair that her husband has the sole right to make all the major decisions, for she's witnessed her father's role in the household. And this is why she thinks it's only right:

"You be under your father's care and then under your husband's, men havin' the stronger brains. Woman hath not a very strong mind, you know. I heard tell of a lass oncet, she father taught her t' read and write. Well, one day her goest mad 'n' strangles her daughter, her did. Them at court said 'twas the learnin' of readin' 'n' writtin' done it, destroyed she brain, it not so strong's a man's brain, couldn't take the strain, yer see."

A woman's time, as she tells it, is taken up with doing much the same kinds of chores day after day.

There's the constant cooking, cleaning up babies, tending to the little ones when they're sick. Added to this is the need to take care of the herb garden, as well as help out at spring planting and harvest time. Then there's the drying, smoking, and pickling of meats and fish, pounding up the corn into meal with mortar and pestle, and butter and cheese making. Women are usually the ones who make the beer, too.

But none of this seems to bother Mary, and she says there are joyful moments while tending to her chores. "I like workin' in the garden of a quiet mornin' when the sun's just coom up and everythin' seems so new and fresh. I like milkin' cows, too, that be a very soothin' thing."

The menfolk work hard as well, but since they do not have the responsibility of taking care of little ones, they have more time for visiting and gossiping. What's more, they can break up the sameness of their daily routine by going hunting or fishing on occasion. Women are not allowed to engage in those activities, for who'd take care of hearth and home?

But there are festivities which the women and menfolk share together, of which the most joyous is a wedding. Understandably, weddings are not frequent in this small community. When one does take place, it's a daylong celebration and everyone in the village participates.

What better way to know what such a gala occasion is like than to have Mary describe her own wedding day to us?

"Oh, there were days and days of preparation. Of makin' food for the weddin' feast, for me to make me weddin' dress. 'Twere a bodice [a tight-fitting, sleeveless waist] mooch like I'm wearin' now. 'Twere an old one and soomat faded, so we did redye it with woad [indigo] so it come to blue, true blue for constancy. And havin' an orange skirt, I did embroider it with orange and green. Took me a week t' finish of it.

"The weddin' day did start very early. 'Round about cockcrow they did come and play me me weddin' song. 'Tis a song to wake up the bride and welcome her on her final day of maidenhood. Then we went out gatherin' garlands for me, me bridesmaids, for the groom's men and for the groom to wear. So that most all the mornin' we were very busy tendin' to sooch. And I were shakin' all that time, most all day. Could hardly do a thing. And, of course, there was the daily chores to do that mornin', too. Sooch as milkin', makin' breakfast, and all. Though me, I couldn't eat a thing, I were that nervous, I were. For you get used to havin' parents and brothers and sisters about. And then to go livin' with just one person instead, 'tis a hard choice. Especially 'cause we be a very close family.

"Now, that mornin', too, we had dancin'. We had maiden dances and we had a very pretty one called the 'ribbon dance.' It be one of me favorite dances.

"We women stayed at this end of the village, nearby the sea. Now Robert, he did live with the Standishes, the captain, at the top of the hill. So we did not see each other durin' the mornin'. We're not supposed to see each other 'til the weddin', for it would be very bad luck for the groom to gaze upon his bride or she to do that to him.

"At the other end of the village the men did high-jinks, did play pranks upon the groom. They did toss Robert in a blanket. Then they did toss him without a blanket. And did badger him about it bein' his final day of freedom and sooch like.

"I didn't get dressed for the weddin' 'til about one of the clock. Oh, but first I couldn't find me stockings and then we couldn't tie up the garters. Me poor mother, she were so flustered that when it came time to pin on me stomacher [separate center piece worn over the bodice], she kept pinnin' me instead. Oh, and then I had to do me hair. Normally we wear it up, but for this you put it down. For the last day of bein' a maiden you wear it down and adorn it with a chaplet [wreath] of flowers and herbs. Things like marjoram for grace and sage for long life.

"Just before two of the clock we had a procession .and did come up the hill at the sound of the horn of .Jonathan Brewster, he bein' a fine trumpeter, he be. So we did proceed up and got Robert at Captain Standish's. Then Robert, me little sister Ann, me friend Constance, Francis Billington, Edward Dotey, he bein' the best friend of the groom, and, of course, me dear friends Patience and Priscilla, who were me brides-maids, we did all proceed down to the goovnor's house.

"'Twas there we get married, in his yard. It be a civil weddin', for they follows the Dutch custom here, the Separatists do, and have a civil weddin'. They feelin'

Wedding ceremony

that is has more to do with law than it do with the Lord.

"And so we was married by goovnor, who did pronounce us man and wife as witness to our plight and troth and in accordance with common law. The goovnor, he did break the bridecake over me head. Not on me head, but held it over me head and break it apart and threw the pieces out to the crowd. For it be a very nice thing to gather up a piece of the bridecake and put it under your pillow and dream of whom you're to wed. Oh, and there were Indians at the weddin', too, bein' invited by goovnor.

"Then there came the scatterin' of wheat for thot Robert and me should have many children. Then, as soon as Robert and me came to the garden gate, I knew it were goin' to happen for it happens at every weddin'. Me garters, what be holdin' up the stockin's, are a great prize for the young men of the village. So I knew they were goin' to chase me for to take me garters from me.

"Now as soon as Robert had got me to the gate, he did try to block it, for I did tell him I were goin' to run and give them a merry chase. Then Edward, as grooms-man, did decide to start off the chase and did yell for a'catchin' of me garters. And so I did take off like a rabbit 'round the house. They did not expect me to go 'round the house so they wasn't ready for thot. Though some did chase after me and some did go 'round the other way to catch me. But I then did take off through Bradford field and almost all the way to the Alden house 'fore I were caught. And me garters was taken off, which were worn by the young men the entire day as favors of the bride.

"I were then brought back to the kissin' circle, for I must kiss all the men in the village. And me father gives me the final kiss after I go 'round the circle kissin' everyone in their fashion. But he gave the final kiss for I be goin' to another man.

"Then we did have the 'Beginnin' of the World.' That be a dance here as a way of celebratin' a married couple's new life together. Robert and I did dance in the center while all danced 'round.

"After that came games, songs, more dancin' and

drinkin', and this part of the weddin' is a custom called the 'bride's ale.' For there be a custom in some towns and villages in England for the bride to sell ale to the company and thereby get money to start her new household. But I did not do that. For I gave the ale to all instead. But I must dance with whatever would ask, that bein' part of the custom of the bride's ale, too.

"Then finally, after the games and the dancin' and the eatin' of all the foods, and all the toasts—to the bride, to the groom, to the King, to whatever, so long it be a toast—then came the beddin' ceremony. It bein' a way of the bride and groom settlin' in the village. We did start a procession all the way up at the redoubt [fort] and then to me family's house for we be stayin' there for the winter.

"I were carried over the threshhold and the beddin' ceremony started. We got down to our chemise, or shift, and were put to bed. The young folk of the village, what 'course are not yet married, take our stockin's and they do sit to the back, at the foot of the bed, and we're sittin' up. And they do take turns throwin' the stockin's over their shoulder. If a sock, thrown by a girl do hit the bride, or a boy to hit the groom, that be a sign of their speedy marriages. Both Francis and me sister Ann did that. So I 'spect they'll be married in a year's time, not necessarily to each other, 'course.

"When everyone did leave, Robert and I did drink what's called the 'sack posset,' for 'tis also the marriage custom. Many folk in England do drink posset. You might call it an evenin' drink right 'fore you go to bed, it bein' cream and eggs. A sack posset hath sack in it,

Wedding feast

which is usually ale. There be a good pint of it and you must needs that he drink half and the bride drinks what's left. But Robert, he took just a wee sip and I had to finish all the rest. I don't think I'll be wantin' to eat for another few days.

"Oh weddin's be a wonderful occasion for us here. Maybe more so for the guests than the bride and groom. So I do be hopin' that, come next spring, there be one, maybe two. And mayhap me sister Ann and Francis be one of the bridal couples."

CHAPTER 11

Farewell to Yesterday's America

Yes, your visit has come to an end. It's time to return to the world of today. Short though your stay has been, I hope you now know that, despite the gap in time, despite differences in religious beliefs, customs, and life-styles, people are essentially the same. Whether they live in the seventeenth or twentieth century, they're neither better nor worse, neither more nor less happy.

You may have decided that the food the settlers ate was inferior to what Americans eat today. It may not have seemed as varied or as tasty. But much of today's food is far less nutritious and some of it is actually harmful. That's because of the use of chemical preservatives, artificial flavoring, and color dyes.

The settlers' lack of indoor plumbing, central heating, and electricity probably seemed a serious drawback. No automatic washing machine or dishwashers, no electric lights, toasters, can openers, and such. But to supply all the power needed for such comforts has caused the erection of nuclear power plants all over to-day's America. Most scientists believe that these plants are already contaminating the locales where they're situated with hazardous fallout and causing a rise in cancer among the people close by. That alone is a terrible price to pay for "easier living."

When we visited with Captain Standish on the gun deck and inspected the cannons, they may have seemed like toys compared to the weapons which exist today. Nuclear weapons are located all over the Western World, and should they ever be used, it could mean the end of all living matter. That's a frightful price to pay for national safety.

The fact that the people of Plimoth subjected those who broke the law to being "set in the stocks," to public whippings, to branding, and even to hanging may have struck you as quite cruel and barbaric. But modern America's supposedly more humane punishment of criminal behavior doesn't seem to be very effective.

I've tried to give you the true picture of what life was like for what are now called the "Pilgrims." As a result, I hope you now see that, though their life was often harsh and had many disadvantages, today's world has its drawbacks too: energy crises, economic problems, rising crime, and so on. Thus I hope you are leaving Plimoth Plantation with the ability to appreciate life then and now without judging one as better or worse than the other, but merely as different.

And by the way, now that you know so much about Plimoth Plantation, you might wish to visit it on your own. It is, after all, a real place. And you may find many other things of interest there which we didn't have time to explore.

About the Author

Robert H. Loeb, Jr., was born in New York City and grew up in Switzerland, Arizona, and New York. After attending Brown and Columbia universities, he pursued a variety of writing-related careers, from magazine editing to setting up his own mail-order book publishing business. With nearly twenty books to his credit, Mr. Loeb now lives in northern Connecticut close to the settings of both *New England Village* and *Meet the* Real *Pilgrims.*